The Phygital Church

Using Social Ministry to Make Disciples

Angelique Jordan-Byrd

© 2021 The Phygital Church: Using Social Ministry to Make Disciples by Angelique Jordan-Byrd

All rights reserved. This book or parts thereof may not be reproduced in any form without prior written permission of the publisher except as provided by United States of America Copyright Law. Send permission requests to:

Center Street Publishing, LLC

P.O. Box 438534

Chicago, IL

ISBN: 978-1-7372233-0-6

The Phygital Church

Dedication

I dedicate this book to all who lost their lives during the COVID-19 pandemic. And to my cherished friends who made their transition during this time: Reginald Relf and Jana Gillespie-Reeves. They will forever hold a space in my heart.

> *Jesus said to her, "I am the resurrection and the life. The one who believes in me will live, even though they die, and whoever lives by believing in me will never die.*
>
> *John 11: 25 - 26 NIV*

I also dedicate this book to clergy across the nation who have endured the impact of the pandemic. You adjusted your ministries to care for God's people while grieving that you could not comfort the beloved community in person. It is my prayer this book will help you move forward embracing ministry in a Phygital environment.

Lastly, I want to acknowledge the support of my three amazing children, editor, clergy friends, Sorority Sisters, and the Jordan Family. I appreciate all of those who came along this journey with me as I remained obedient to the Spirit. Thank you.

Table of Contents

INTRODUCTION	1
THE PHYGITAL ENVIRONMENT	4
WHY PHYGITAL?	6
SOCIAL MINISTRY	18
SOCIAL MEDIA PLATFORMS	24
SOCIAL MEDIA STRATEGY	46
SOCIAL MEDIA ANALYTICS	51
SOCIAL CONTENT	56
SOCIAL MEDIA ADVERTISING	66
NEW MINISTRY POSITIONS FOR THE PHYGITAL CHURCH	72
OTHER PHYGITAL RESOURCES	77
REFLECTIONS AND CALL TO ACTION	81
ENDNOTES	103

Forward

Recent events have changed the way we communicate and introduced new platforms for communication with the masses. Nowadays, we can minister healing and hope in a space that reaches millions of people. We refer to this space as a Phygital environment, which allows for conducting ministry in our **phy**sical churches and the di**gital** domain. This book will help clergy be intentional with navigating and utilizing the digital space to achieve church goals.

Introduction

Matthew 28: 19-20 states, "Therefore go and make disciples of all nations, baptizing them in the name of the Father and of the Son and of the Holy Spirit and teaching them to obey everything I have commanded you."

The pandemic changed many things – how we shop, work, celebrate birthdays and holidays, attend worship service, care for one another, and how we communicate. Communication is an integral part of our connectivity and serves as the method we share almost everything. Communication is also essential to the Body of Christ because it represents how we create communities that allow us to support one another along life's journey.

The pandemic presented clergy with challenges never faced before. While our country was dealing with a deadly virus, our means of providing care for one another changed.
Physical touch was no longer an option, and gathering on Sunday was prohibited. For most members, Sunday Worship Service had been where they went to build their faith for the

week. Sunday worship was where parishioners went to find comfort to deal with daily challenges. Unfortunately, the pandemic and the requisite safety recommendations brought everything to an abrupt halt.

Safety guidelines required clergy to become innovative and make quick changes to overcome the limitations presented by the pandemic. These changes forced Pastors into a new way of ministry.

Clergy became creative by streaming services on social media, creating podcasts, having online bible studies, sharing worship videos, and organizing drive-in church services. It did not take long before clergy began to recognize the benefits of being in a digital environment. The use of social media expanded clergy's ministerial reach worldwide, providing access to people ordinarily out of their reach.

For some churches, their online attendance exceeded their pre-pandemic attendance. Deacon Jeffery Humphrey, of Mount Ebal Missionary Baptist Church in Joliet, Illinois, states *"Going from live in-person service to virtual service has actually been beneficial as far as the Gospel being spread. On a regular Sunday morning we may have anywhere from 50 to 100 people who attend service. Our first week of going virtual we had over 700 people watching our service."* According to the Barna Group, amid the pandemic, 44% of church leaders said their virtual attendance was higher than their typical Sunday attendance.[1]

People throughout the nation began to turn to their faith to endure the unpredictability of the pandemic. "Nearly three-in-ten U.S. adults say the outbreak has boosted their faith; about four-in-ten say it has tightened family bonds."[2] In the process, relationships and friendships emerged by way of social media platforms.

The pandemic has taught us many lessons. Among them are the importance of being in community with one another, caring for one another, and growing ministry beyond the four walls of churches, to name a few. These are lessons to be carried into the new season on which we will embark.

The Phygital Environment

Many people have stated, we will never go back to church as we knew it. What was once considered normal will no longer be. We will need to create a "new normal" as it relates to ministry.

Post-pandemic, many churches will navigate back inside their church buildings. However, we should be mindful not everyone will return immediately, if at all. In addition, there have been connections made online that will need to be maintained with people on social media who are outside the Body of Christ. For these reasons, churches should consider ministering in a "Phygital" environment.

A Phygital environment requires us to be active in a physical location while maintaining a digital presence. Churches will be sharing God's word in their "physical" church as well as in the "digital" space. It is imperative to note the Phygital environment is not just streaming worship services online. The Phygital environment will require clergy to remain intentional about engaging in the digital space.

> *"It is imperative to note the Phygital environment is not just streaming worship services online. It will require clergy to remain intentional about engaging in the digital space."*

The pandemic has shifted us to platforms that allow us to enlarge our mission field. God positioned the church to broaden our territory and minister in a Phygital environment; this helps to leave no one behind.

In the Phygital setting, we can share and uplift people in our physical church and digital spaces. The Phygital makes it possible to bring what we are doing offline to an online environment simultaneously and consistently. Depending on the context, Phygital ministry can also include connecting the digital space with your physical space.

Why Phygital?

As we enter the following season, some may wonder "why" they should continue in the digital space once they return to their sanctuaries. During the pandemic, social media became the outlet for many churches.

Suppose your organization used this medium to reach and encourage viewers by posting videos, memes, or inspirational messages. In that case, it is essential to maintain these connections.

One of the common concerns against a Phygital Church is the belief people will not attend the physical church. Ministering in a Phygital environment should be approached as a "both/and" option and not an "either/or."

Church members who appreciate being in the sanctuary will continue to do so. However, some congregants cannot be in the physical space, possibly due to health or safety concerns, limited mobility, or personal preference. Some people may prefer Social Ministry (the use of Social Media for ministry, which we will further discuss in the following section).

Sharing your worship service online helps those who cannot attend. Virtual attendees can feel a part of the worship experience. They can see and participate in worship services or bible study along with other congregants. For some, it can remove the feeling of isolation. Phygital provides the opportunity to reach more people and should not be thought of as limiting.

> *"The Phygital environment is an opportunity to expand your ministry."*

There is also a belief that the older generation has no desire to be in a Phygital Church because of the need to engage with technology. Pastor Adam Harmon, of Central Christian Church in Danville, Illinois, shared of the experience with his congregation:

> *"I think it is really easy to generalize and say that older generations are technology avoidant. Instead, I believe that the different generations place value differently on things like money, saving, and practicality. Although much of my church was not familiar with the technology; when Covid hit we realized that a vast majority of us had Facebook accounts. Streaming the service through Facebook allowed people to stay connected. It is the older generations value of being connected and still attending church that then allowed them to see value in the technology that could make that happen. Once the technology was being used, even though it was very rough at first, people were able to see that people who have not attended in a long time were tuning in, people who had moved away were tuning in, and people who just ran across us online were tuning in. The*

> *value of sustaining that technology then became intrinsically connected with the value of the church experience. An experience that the older generations care about greatly.*
>
> *These are just some of my thoughts around our situation here at Central. Ultimately this process has also opened the door to talking more about how we measure success in the church. When worship is not only limited to a physical building but is also online; the way we look at numbers and participation, and what we view as success has to change."*

Pastor Harmon's congregation was able to see beyond the technology requirements once they experienced a benefit of The Phygital Church, staying connected. For the older generation at Central Christian Church in Danville, these connections were integral to the worship experience and outweighed any obstacles with the use of technology.

Lastly, some believe participants cannot "experience" the worship service in a digital environment. This is to imply we did not experience the move of God in 2020-2021. That is simply not true! If we honestly believe God is omnipresent, we know God's spirit can also reside in digital and physical spaces.

I am a witness, as I have heard the stories and have attended online devotion services with those who experienced the move of God. I believe God functions in all aspects of our lives and is present everywhere. We are, after all, referencing the same God who made the moon and the stars and *spoke* things into existence!

We have the Internet and the technology we use today because God led someone to create these tools to help us spread the Gospel. God did not command us to stay within the four walls of our churches.

Jesus and the Disciples went out and met people where they were to share the Good News. The Phygital space provides you with an opportunity to meet people in the digital universe, yes, where God also resides.

Now that we have addressed Phygital Church concerns let us review why being in the Phygital space is beneficial for churches. When we approach the Phygital Church as "both/and," the two environments work together beautifully.

The Phygital Church allows clergy to utilize online resources to help meet the church's goals. We all continue to strive to introduce the Gospel and make Disciples. Social Ministry will enable us to "go" even further than our sanctuaries on Sunday mornings. If you are interested in sharing the Gospel with youth, you are bound to find them in the digital space!

If your goal is simply to create awareness for your church, the digital arena has tools available to help expand your reach. When we are intentional and strategic about engaging online, we reinforce the actions occurring in our physical churches to accomplish church goals.

Most people engaging in Social Ministry will view Sunday worship or interact with their church via a computer or smartphone. According to Backlinko, 99% of social media users engage with websites or apps through a mobile device.[3] Pew Research tells us 97% of Americans have cellphones, and 85% of that total have smartphones.[4] Mobile technology provides an excellent opportunity to reach millions of people who may tune in through their smartphone, a device most people do not leave home without.

Over the past several years, church attendance has been decreasing across the nation. Some churches attributed this decrease to generations no longer being believers or interested in worship services.

Notwithstanding, these numbers may be lower because generations have used different outlets to build their faith. As a result, we must consider that church attendance is not only decreasing; it is also decentralizing.

> "... we must consider that church attendance is not only decreasing; it is also decentralizing."

People are finding new mediums to read scriptures and explore Christianity. There are a great majority of people who participate in different television ministries and others that worship online.

When we look specifically at millennials, there have been discussions regarding the decrease in numbers among those who attend indoor church services. The Barna Group conducted a study about millennials, faith, and technology. One of their conclusions states,

> *"For church leaders, the data point to lots of opportunities to engage Millennials spiritually online. Two trends converge: Millennials leaving the church and Millennials taking their faith discussions and explorations online. One of the most positive trends among Millennials is that they want a holistically integrated faith into all areas of life –*

> *including their technology. How the church acknowledges and engages the digital domain — and teaches faithfulness in real-life to young adults as well — will determine much about its long-term effectiveness among Millennials."[5]*

The above is one example of a generation utilizing the digital space as a medium for spiritual growth. So, if we want to continue to reach people with the Gospel, we must be present where they reside.

> *"... if we want to continue to reach people with the Gospel, we must be present where they reside."*

The findings also relate to the importance of teaching millennials faithfulness in real life as well. The Phygital Church will recognize the importance of being in both spaces consistently. Thus, this book is for you if your church recognizes the importance of ministry in the physical and digital space concurrently.

The physical limitations presented by the pandemic caused a sudden shift into the virtual space. As this was a new arena for many, Pastors moved online to platforms that were easy to navigate.

This book will help you determine which platforms are best for your church, given the goals you have set forth to accomplish. The following pages will assist churches and ministries with navigating strategically in the virtual space.

This book aims to teach you how the virtual space can become an extension of your physical space and how to bring the two locations together to accomplish your church's goals. But doing so requires planning, and each section will help you develop a strategic social media plan for your church.

Before we begin our journey, let us do some groundwork. The following worksheet will help you capture yearly goals and what you know about our congregation.

Pre-Planning Worksheet

A. Write down three of your church's yearly goals.

    1.

    2.

    3.

B. Identify demographics and characteristics of your current congregation:

    1. Gender (% male/female)
        a. Male:
        b. Female:

    2. Ages (%)
        a. 5 - 17
        b. 18 – 29
        c. 30 – 49
        d. 50 – 64
        e. 65+

    3. Their proximity to your church:

    4. Interests:

    5. Other identifiable characteristics or demographics:

Pre-Planning Worksheet cont.

C. Write down attributes that best describe your church:

    1.

    2.

    3.

    4.

    5.

D. Utilizing the information above, write two brief statements that best describe your church:

    1.

    2.

Social Ministry

It is essential to understand how the digital space allows for Social Ministry to reinforce the efforts of your physical church and the benefits of using social media. Social Ministry occurs when we use social media platforms for Ministry. You utilize Social Ministry for discipleship when you share worship services, prayer videos, and scriptural posts, etc.

Unlike major corporations, churches have been late adopters with using social media. Some churches were late adopters to social media platforms because they envisioned them as sites where people gathered to talk and share funny memes. They did not realize the benefits social media provides when you are strategic and intentional with the information you share.

Using social media platforms, we, the church, can carry out ministry in the virtual space. We can proactively reach out and care for one another on any of these platforms. We can share the Gospel, offer encouragement, provide hope, support, and be attentive to each other's needs. Social Ministry is another means for us to do as the Great Commission has called us to do, to *go*.

According to Hootsuite, there are 3.96 billion people on social media. Using these platforms for Social Ministry allows us to go, teach, reach, and make disciples almost everywhere.

> *"According to Hootsuite, there are 3.96 billion people on social media. Using these platforms for Social Ministry allows us to go, teach, reach, and make disciples almost everywhere."*

At the onset of the pandemic, churches shifted from worshiping in their churches to Social Ministry. Churches throughout the country began streaming or video recording their worship services for viewers.

Social Media platforms became inundated with positive, uplifting, and encouraging posts to help people navigate during this significant crisis that impacted the entire world. It was through Social Ministry many received their hope and faith to endure.

Trust is a critical component for establishing relationships. When we are in a community with one another in an online and physical environment, it fosters trust. These established relationships may open the door for people to hear the truth about God and be the encouragement needed for viewers to attend the in-person Worship Service at your church.

Social Ministry also allows churches to reach people all over the world, any time of day. Most physical churches have Sunday Worship and Wednesday Bible Study. The Phygital space enables you to expand the hours of your church.

When these worship services, and small group meetings, are shared online, viewers can watch any day of the week. Those awake at 2 a.m. from anxiety can find a worship video on YouTube addressing that topic.

The Phygital Church 21

While the church doors may be closed, your Social Ministry doors will always be opened to help people in their time of need. Ministry happens when people click on your videos, read your posts, or when you interact with your audience online, not just on Sunday mornings or Wednesday evenings.

Social Ministry Worksheet

If you have already initiated your Social Ministry, take a few moments to document some baseline information before moving forward.

A. Compile a list of each of the Social Media Platforms your church is currently utilizing:
    1.
    2.
    3.

B. What is the frequency in which you are interacting with your audience?
    1. Daily
    2. Weekly
    3. Monthly

C. What types of posts are you currently sharing the most?
    1. Text Posts
    2. Graphic Posts
    3. Pre-recorded videos
    4. Live Stream Videos
    5. Other:

D. Categorize the type of content you are sharing on social media and write a percentage for each one.
    1. Informative
    2. Promotional
    3. Inspiring
    4. Entertaining
    5. Other:

Social Media Platforms

Myspace was one of the first Social Media platforms started in 2003. Since that time, platforms have evolved and provided many features to encourage interaction. Today, other Social Media platforms exist, including YouTube, Facebook, Instagram, Twitter, Pinterest, LinkedIn, and the growing popular TikTok.

Social Media platforms are where people create community. Another critical objective of Social Media is to build relationships. Once people can establish trust on these platforms, relationships can flourish.

This section will provide an overview of the major social media platforms and the people who reside on them. You can begin to determine where your target audience can be reached to start establishing a community.

YouTube

YouTube, founded in 2005, is one of the two most prominent social media platforms (as it relates to the percentage of U.S. adults who use the site). Acquired by Google in 2006, YouTube is widely known for video sharing.

During the pandemic, churches created YouTube channels to share worship videos. You can save videos for people to review and reference at any time. However, try to refrain from using the platform as a place to just "store" your videos. Consider it as an outlet to reach more people with God's word.

If you are a church that decides to post videos on YouTube, it is essential to remember this site is one of the largest search engines. Most people visiting YouTube are in search of an answer to a question. Their search will usually lead with: How to, What is, etc. Take advantage of this knowledge and optimize your video titles by forming questions, creating short titles, and keeping keywords upfront.

For example, a sermon regarding faith in trying times could be titled "How to grow your faith in challenging times." Changing the title does not alter your sermon message; it simply allows your material to be more accessible on YouTube.

Review analytics to determine if your title is adequate. If you find viewers clicking off within the first 10 seconds, consider updating your title, as viewers may not have discovered what they were looking for.

Viewers on YouTube prefer authentic videos where the presenter displays expertise on a specific subject matter of interest. Other videos may include your worship service. Creating videos with speakers who talk directly into the camera in a conversational tone will also perform well on this site.

According to the chart below, approximately 81% of U.S. adults are accessing the platform. The daily average of time spent on YouTube is 40 minutes.[6] People are searching for answers, and we have the one solution that will solve many of their problems. We just need to have a presence on the platform to share it.

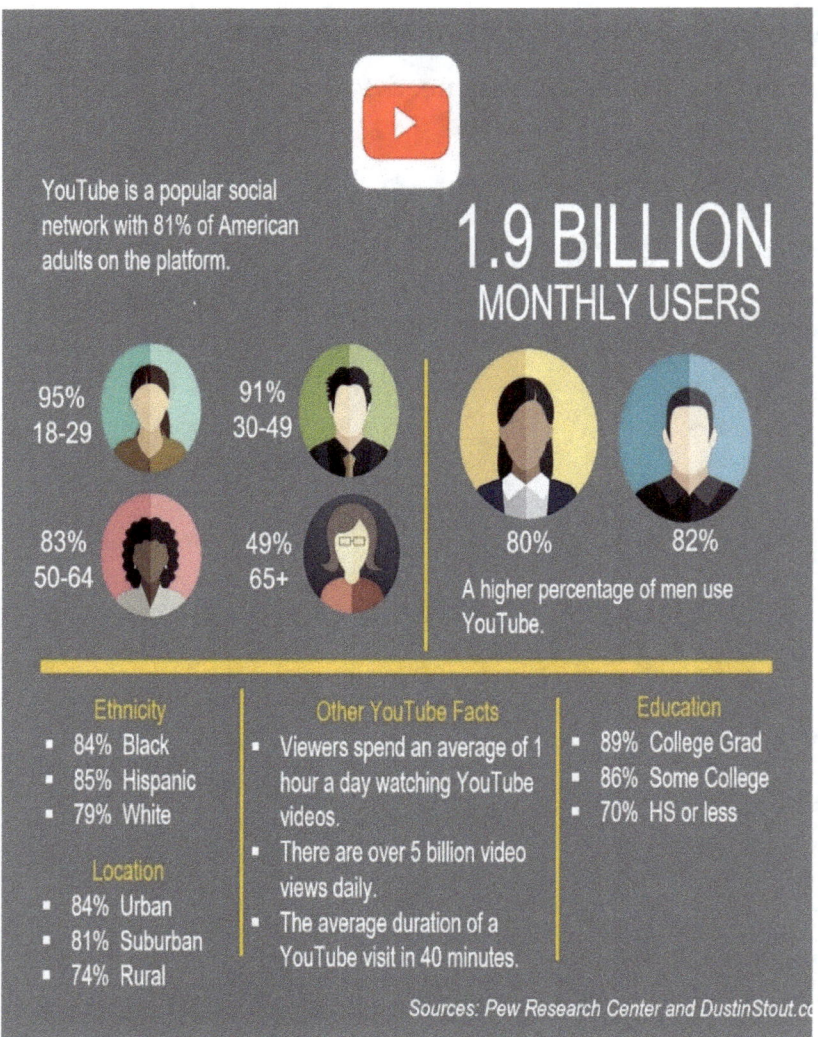

Facebook

Facebook is a platform for making connections. It was created in 2004 and has grown to approximately 2.4 billion monthly users, as shown in the following chart.

Engagement on this platform is driven by a wide range of content. Facebook posts consist of text, images, video, Facebook Stories, and the opportunity to engage via Facebook Live.

Facebook has both Facebook Pages and Facebook Groups. Facebook Pages allow you to connect and share important information regarding your church on the page's profile. Churches are encouraged to fully complete the details in their profile. Be sure to include the address for your church and the hours of your worship service and other weekly gatherings.

Like a website home page, your Facebook page is the first impression people will get of your church. The cover photo is an excellent place to show an engaging hi-resolution image. This image can be changed, and image modification is helpful when communicating various activities or church services. Page Administrators control the sharing of content on a Facebook Page.

Facebook Groups are a great place to create community. Groups allow you to interact with people who share the same interests. Facebook Groups can help grow your ministries: Women's Ministry, Men's Ministry, or other small groups.

Creating a group from your Facebook page connects the group to your organization. It provides space for members of the group to interact and support one another.

There are three types of Facebook Groups: public, closed, and secret. Anyone can see the content and join a public group. You can search and find a closed group. However, you have to request to join or be added by a current member to view the content. Lastly, a secret group cannot be found in a search, and content is only visible to those in the group. A friend/member has to invite you to join a secret group.

Many churches create closed groups because people can locate them and request to join. Unlike a Facebook Page, a Facebook Group allows members to post directly. You do not have to be an Administrator to share, which helps foster conversations.

In a Phygital space, churches may stream their worship services or utilize the Facebook Live feature. However, it is vital to have someone online to engage with those attending service virtually.

Just as relationships are formed in the church building, they are also established in the virtual space. Having the same person manage the online service will provide continuity and help with building relationships.

When interacting on Facebook, generate your content from your church's Facebook page. While clergy may prefer to use their personal Facebook page, keep in mind visitors who want to find your page will likely search using the name of your church. They may not be aware of the Pastor's name or Worship Leader's name.

Using your church's Facebook Page allows new visitors to quickly find you on the platform. If you decide to use your personal page, be sure to share the content with your church's page or vice versa. The key is to ensure you are sharing information from the church's Facebook page.

If you consider a presence on Facebook, it is helpful to know the people on that platform. Facebook is prevalent across all demographics.

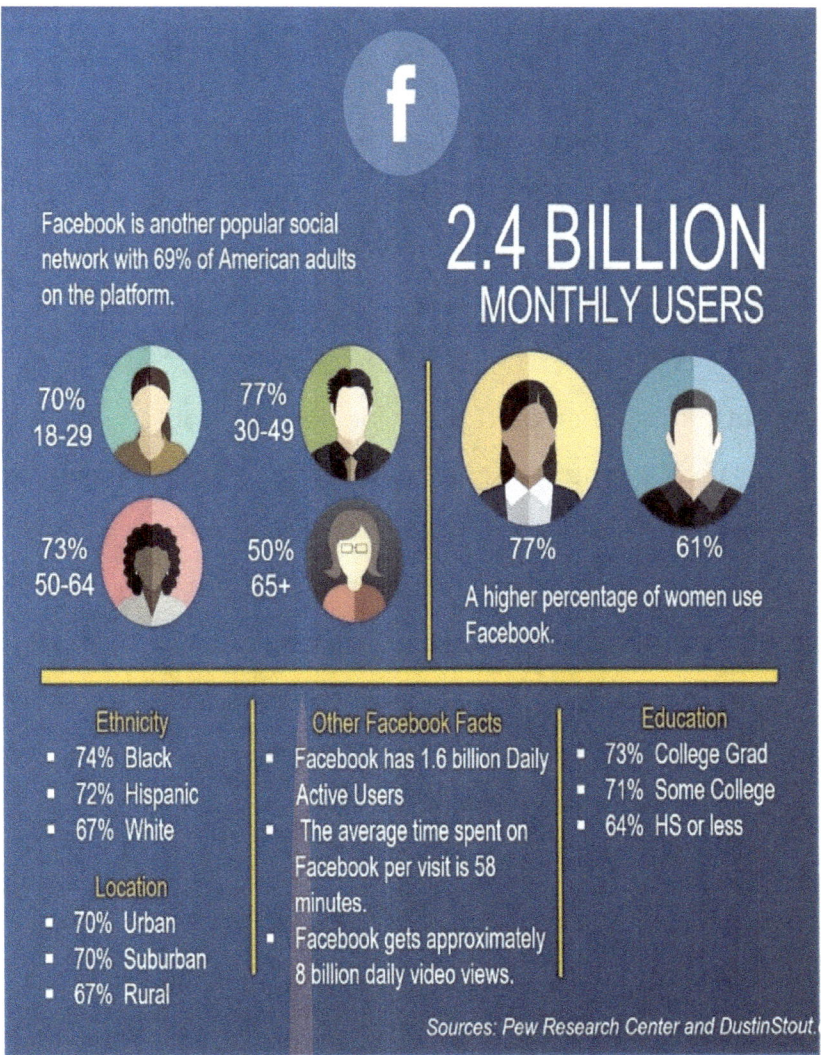

Instagram

Instagram is a fun, light-hearted platform for sharing content. Established in 2010, it has grown to include more than photos. Members of this platform are now sharing engaging videos via Instagram Stories, Reels, and I.G.T.V.

Instagram is another platform that permits you to provide details about your organization. Take advantage of completing the short bio section (150 characters) to communicate a tagline or a critical insight about your church. You may also add your website address as a clickable link, a contact name, and additional social media accounts to share content across platforms. There are several areas to engage with your audience on Instagram:

> *Feed:* where you will like and comment on posts
> *Profile:* where people engage with your posts
> *Stories:* where you can engage through short stories that disappear in 24 hours or ask questions and tag others to see your content

I.G.T.V.: where you can create longer-form videos for up to 10 minutes. However, shorter is better.

Search Tab: where you will locate posts to engage with

According to Pew Research, Instagram is a popular site for teens ages 13 to 17, with 72% saying they use the site.[7] If your ministry wishes to reach this audience and the other demographics listed on the following chart, consider using Instagram in your Social Media Strategy.

Clergy are also encouraged to share from the church's Instagram account. If you decide to create an account for your Youth Ministry, use the name of your church. Again, it is best to refrain from creating it under the name of the Youth Leader. The church name is more recognizable, and you do not risk losing history for your church if there is a change in Youth Ministers.

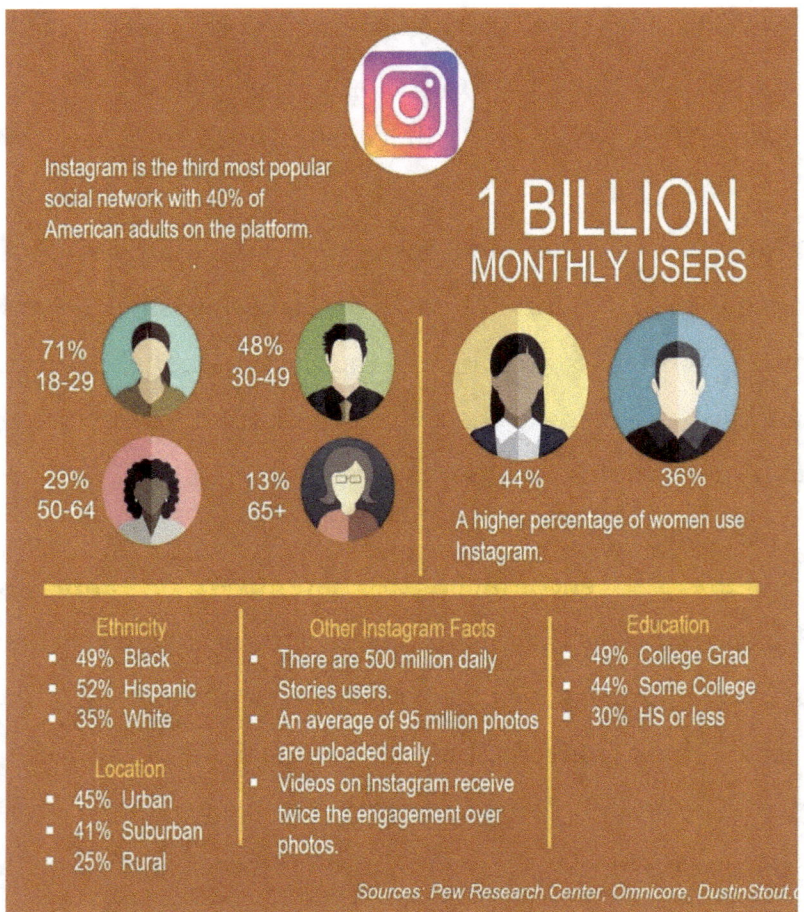

Twitter

Twitter was initially created in 2006 to share news and is famous as the site of short messages. Tweets are comprised of short messages with no more than 280 characters. Twitter is a fast-moving site; tweets move quickly, post multiple times daily and consider re-posting high-performing content.

Twitter allows you to add information regarding your organization in the profile section as well. The biography field allows for 160 characters and should be used to share essential information about your church. The media gallery will allow you to upload images/videos. Take advantage of this opportunity by populating the field with images of your church, congregation, or other photos or videos that represent your church.

Community is created on Twitter when users participate in conversations related to the goals or interests of your church. The use of hashtags is also standard on this platform (as well as Instagram, TikTok, and YouTube). Hashtags are keywords or phrases written without space and include the pound sign in front, i.e., #phygital. Hashtags help people find your posts more easily. In addition, they help you reach the target audience who is interested in your content.

Therefore, it is essential to ensure hashtags are relevant and include words people may use in their search. When using a hashtag, you should limit the number to two or three in a post.

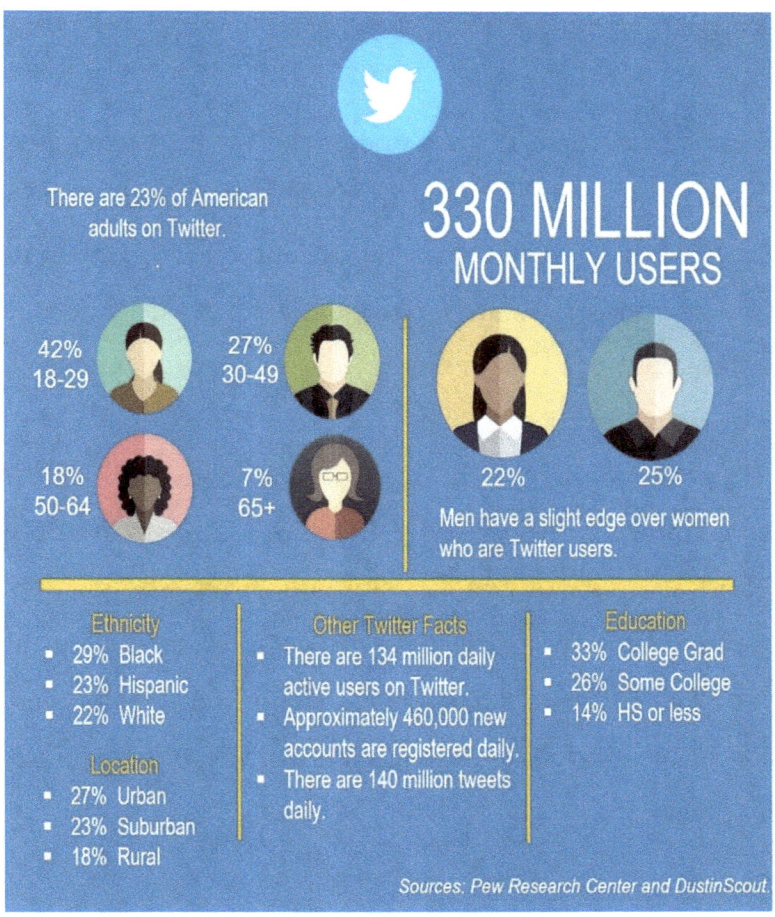

TikTok

Created in 2016, TikTok is one of the fastest-growing social media platforms.[8] As of July 2021, TikTok increased the length of its videos from 60 seconds to three minutes.[9] TikTok videos are categorized into dance, education, self-care, inspirational quotes, and prayer, to name a few.

This platform is where teens and young adults reside. According to Oblero, 62% of U.S. TikTok users are between 10 and 29 years of age. "A new study has shown younger people ages four to fifteen spend an average of 80 minutes per day on the app."[10] TikTok is a site with high engagement, and because videos are displayed quickly, they can achieve great reach.

Hashtags are also commonly used on TikTok. There are many to select from to find content. The algorithm will show your content to people who engage with similar tags. You have a good chance of gaining followers if you are active on

TikTok. The greater your involvement, the greater are the chances for your account to gain followers.

This platform is where prayer videos and testimonials are compelling. Creating a one- to three-minute prayer video provides you with the opportunity to pray with millions of people daily.

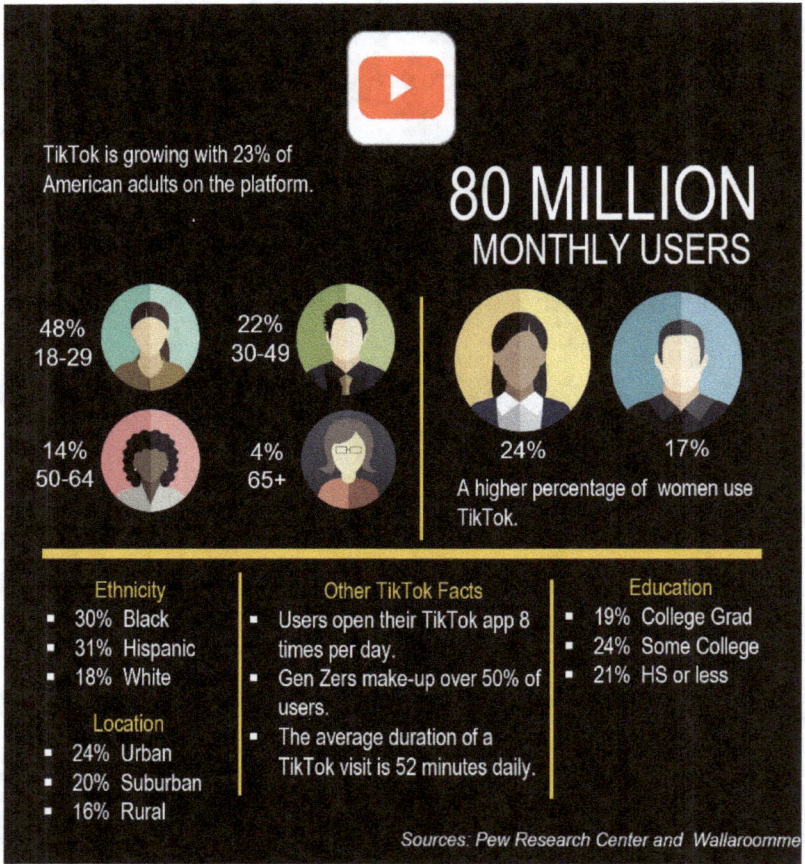

Now that you have reviewed each social media platform, reflect on your church goals and target audience. Determine which social media platform(s) would be best to create a community. The key here is *quality over quantity*. It is not necessary to be on every platform.

While consistency in messages is encouraged, try to avoid sharing the same creative across all social media platforms simultaneously. If your followers notice the same content, it gives them a reason to stop following you on some of your accounts.

Social Media Platforms Worksheet

Now that you have read about the various social media platforms answer the questions below.

1. Reflecting on the demographics of your congregation, which platform(s) do you believe best reflect your community?

2. Which social media platform(s) is well-suited for reaching your yearly goals?

3. Which features on these platforms will be best for sharing your content?

4. Depending on how you plan to share your worship services online, which platforms are most appropriate for your set-up?

Answer if you answered #2 with YouTube:

5. Because YouTube is a significant search engine, take some of the church's previous sermons and convert them to SEO headlines for YouTube.

    Remember to write the titles in the form of questions
    a.
    b.
    c.

6. Identify topics related to your yearly goals that are appropriate for creating videos speaking directly into the camera.
    a.
    b.
    c.

Social Media Strategy

As previously mentioned, Social Ministry allows you to reach your church goals in the online space. Developing a social media strategy will ensure you complement the physical church's efforts in the online environment.

When Pastors transitioned to social media at the onset of the pandemic, the goal was to go online with their worship service. The platforms selected were driven by convenience and ease. As time continued to pass, many were able to learn how to enhance their online worship services by utilizing chat boxes and perfecting the video experience for their viewers. Time did not allow for an in-depth look at which social media platform was best for your church or plan on how you could still reach your ministry goals in this new environment.

A Social Media Strategy will help ensure your Social Ministry aligns with your yearly church goals. A strategy will also serve as a road map for your online presence.

George Doran is recognized for the concept of S.M.A.R.T. goals. As you begin to establish your strategy, work to create goals that are S.M.A.R.T.:

> *"A Social Media Strategy will help to ensure your Social Ministry is in line with your yearly church goals."*

Specific: Make your goals straightforward. Writing clear and detailed goals increases the chances of people understanding and working towards achieving them together.

Measurable: Your goals should be measurable to determine if they are achieved. What evidence is needed to verify you are making good progress?

Achievable: Be realistic, ensure your goal is one that your church can achieve. Setting an unachievable goal can damper the morale of an online ministry team.

Relevant: Your goals should be in alignment with the direction your church is going. They should share your values and steps that will lead to the achievement of your long-term goals.

Time-Based: Set a timeframe for achieving your objectives.

Your church may be interested in generating online awareness, driving traffic to your church's website, increasing engagement, or building and growing a social ministry community. When you convert generating online awareness to a S.M.A.R.T. goal, you may want to create online awareness of your church in Q1 via Facebook. To accomplish this goal on Facebook, you may consider the following tactics:

1. Create content, consistently schedule posts, and encourage your members to share content.
2. Drive a specific number of mentions with hashtags for Q1.
3. Utilize the boost feature on Facebook to target area codes surrounding your physical location with a digital post about your church in Q1.

These tactics will extend your reach on Facebook and create awareness. You will be able to view analytics to measure your success as well. When establishing your strategy, consider what platforms would be best to connect with the people you are trying to reach. We ultimately want to communicate with anyone outside the Body of Christ. Still, you know which target audience would thrive best at your church.

S.M.A.R.T. Goals Worksheet

Review your yearly church objectives, create quarterly S.M.A.R.T. Goals and steps to accomplish them:

Q1 S.M.A.R.T. Goals:

1.

2.

3.

Q2 S.M.A.R.T. Goals:

1.

2.

3.

Q3 S.M.A.R.T. Goals:

1.

2.

3.

Q4 S.M.A.R.T. Goals:

1.

2.

3.

Social Media Analytics

Social Media Strategies will continue to be a work in progress. There is no one formula to determine your success on these platforms. Reviewing analytics and insights will help you understand if you are meeting your goals and can help you determine areas for improvement. This data will allow you to identify what is working to duplicate efforts for successful Social Ministry.

> *"There is no one formula to determine your success on these platforms. Reviewing analytics and insights will help you understand if you are meeting your goals as well as determine areas for improvement."*

Most social media platforms provide Insights and Analytics. Facebook and Instagram have an integrated A.D. Network. Monitoring analytics will help you realize if people are engaging with your content and what audiences you are reaching. Several of the metrics are indicators for the following:

Page Views: number of times someone viewed your profile

Post Reach: number of people who saw your post

Post Engagement: number of times someone either commented, clicked, shared, or reacted to a post

Page Followers: number of new people following you

Videos: number of times a video is played on your page that exceeded 3 seconds

Impressions: number of times people have an opportunity to review your content

Audience: the people viewing your social media pages

There are metrics to determine your level of success depending on your goal:

Goal	Metric
Awareness	Reach / Impressions
Engagement	Clicks, Reactions

If your goal is to create awareness in Q1, monitor reach and impressions to determine your effectiveness. Analytics will also provide details to help guide your posting. Analytics will indicate the time of day your fans are online the most. You can use this data to advise you when scheduling posts.

Monitor the reach and engagement of your posts. You can determine the posts/content that resonates most with your audience. Scheduling similar content will aid engagement. To solicit comments on your page, post a question to your audience. If you want likes, share engaging photos or videos.

Facebook updates its system frequently. If your church is on Facebook, the Business Suite now provides a section to enter your goals, and Facebook will track the progress.

Social Media Analytics Worksheet

Review the analytics for each of your current social media platforms to answer the following questions.

Audience
1. Who are the fans on your page? (Review age and gender)
2. Who are your followers? (Review age and gender)
3. Write an overall statement about who you are reaching on each social media platform given the above information. (If this is not the audience you want to reach, determine where they reside across the platforms):

Posts
1. What type of posts/content resonates with your audience?
2. What type of posts achieves high engagement?
3. Which posts are generating high reach?

Other
1. What will be the frequency for reviewing analytics?
2. Given your goals, which metrics will you use to determine success?

Social Content

As stated, communication is an integral part of how we connect with one another. Social Media is an excellent platform for making connections and building community. To support these efforts, you should be purposeful about the content being shared. The content shared can be instrumental in helping to meet your Social Ministry goals.

> *"Content facilitates close relationships with your audience when it drives two-way conversations; it is another way to build trust."*

The content in your posts gives viewers insights into your church and a glimpse of your church's personality. Content facilitates close relationships with your audience when it drives two-way conversations; it is another way to build trust.

There are two types of content: created and curated. Created content is just that, content that someone in your organization produces. Curated content is content that already exists from other sources and is shared online. Posting variations of content will help with keeping your audience interested.

Just as it is essential to have an overall Social Media Strategy, a Content Strategy will guide the content shared to meet your goals. Consider these factors when determining your content strategy:

> *Target Audience:* Who are the people you want to reach with your content?
> *Goals:* What do you want to accomplish with your content?
> *Church Voice:* What will be the tone of your content? This tone will be reflective of your church (e.g., warm, welcoming, inclusive).

There are different forms of content to consider when communicating your messages. People share content by way of videos, social media posts, blogs, and photos, etc. Videos can increase engagement. When assessing content engagement, videos receive 74%, images 15%, and text 6%. People view informative videos more than entertaining and promotional videos.[11]

There are various ways churches can create video content without reinventing the wheel. Record Sunday Sermons and create short 1 to 2-minute video snippets that contain main messages. You can share these shorter videos across social media platforms.

Churches may also consider the different types of social media posts: inspirational, informational, conversational, personal, or celebratory. You can determine the post-selection by the characteristics and needs of your target audience. Staying alert to what is happening in your church may guide you on the type of post that will resonate with your online audience. During the pandemic, many posts were inspirational because there was a need, and continues to be a need, to uplift people on these platforms.

Below are examples of effective Social Ministry content.

Prayer: Facebook

Rev. Dr. William E. Crowder Jr. posts a prayer every weekday morning. These prayers are read and shared by many of his followers. This allows for the power of prayer to go forth over social media.

William E Crowder Jr.
August 11 at 3:50 AM ·

Wednesday Prayer... The LORD Is Going To Watch Over You The Rest Of Your life!

Dear God, as we begin a new day, we thank You for the Promise in Isaiah 52:12b that says that the Lord will go ahead of you; yes, the God of Israel will protect you from behind. We trust, Oh God, that You will not only watch our back the rest of 2021 but that You will go ahead of us, You will protect us, You will provide for us and You will help us to prevail over every predicament that we might face in our families and in our future. We know, Oh God, that because You are covering our backside and our frontside we will come through on the other-side. We ask, Oh God, that You help us to know that You will not only walk with us through every challenge that we will face in 2021 but that You will continue to work in us inspite of every challenge we face. We ask, Oh God, that You give us supernatural strength to come through the struggles, prophetic power to overcome the problems and a fearless faith to know that You have us covered from back and the front. We thank You, Oh God, that You are providing backside coverage for Your children today, tomorrow and the rest of our lives. In Jesus Christ Name, It Can And It Will Be Done, Amen!

146   127 Comments 16 Shares

Sunday Service Preview: Instagram

Rev. Melissa Ebken shares her topic for Sunday's Sermon, joy. She asks the question, "How do we celebrate joy in the midst of a pandemic, grief, loss, and suffering?" She then invites viewers to worship together and celebrate joy on Sunday.

Visit the I.G.T.V. channel of illiopolisccdoc to view the video.

Testimonial: TikTok

Herstory333 (Anna Cash) shares a 60 second video. She shares a story of addiction and her spiritual awakening.

Visit https://vm.tiktok.com/ZMJw3Aeq7/ to hear the testimony

Social Content Strategy Worksheet

1. Reflect on the demographics of your church. Define your online target audience and determine who would thrive at your church. (Also, keep in mind, anyone outside the Body of Christ should be included.)

2. Reviewing your S.M.A.R.T. Goals, what key messages/content needs to be shared to achieve your goals?

3. Identify key scriptures that coincide with your above answers:

4. Identify church volunteers who will create content:

5. Identify curated content sources that convey the messages you would like to share:

Social Content Strategy Worksheet cont.

6. What messaging best represents your church? (Church Voice)

7. Using the adjectives from your Pre-Planning Worksheet, create a social media post inviting viewers to visit your church in your church voice. (The statement should describe the personality of your church so viewers know what to expect when they attend.)

Content Calendars

Content Calendars are an excellent way to plan and organize your social content. Developing a content calendar will allow you to schedule your content and keep track of the messages you wish to share. You can list the platform, content, URL, post type, image, format, and time to schedule your posts by platform.

Once you determine the key messages you would like to share online, you can detail the messages on the calendar. Doing so can ensure the content you are sharing is working to meet your objectives. It is also an easy way to plan for content to acknowledge key holidays or coincide with a scheduled sermon series.

Below is a sample of a Content Calendar. You can create one that best fits the information you would like to capture for your church.

Sample Content Calendar

ABC Christian Church

<Day, Date>

Social Media Platform	Content	URL	Type	Image	Format	Time
Facebook						
Facebook						
Facebook						
Instagram						
Instagram						
Instagram						
Twitter						
Twitter						
Twitter						
TikTok						
TikTok						
TikTok						

Social Media Advertising

We have reviewed the various ways Social Ministry, using Social Media, helps the Phygital Church achieve its goals. Posting videos and sharing worship services online is one way to create awareness and share the Gospel. Social Media Advertising is another available option to help achieve church goals.

Social Media ads allow you to extend your reach on social media. Moreover, you can create awareness with a target audience that best resonates with your message or an audience you wish to introduce to your message.

> *"Social Media Advertising is another available option to help achieve church goals."*

There are many details, and the platforms available are robust. At a high level, we will review what is available so you can further explore your options. The key is for you to know these resources are accessible to help you achieve your objectives.

Facebook and Instagram Ads are integrated and operate from Ads Manager to generate ad campaigns. This technology allows you to target the specific audience you are trying to reach by placing your electronic ad, or post, in front of them.

If you know your congregants' demographics, interests, and behaviors, you can create a similar target audience on Facebook. You can select your target audience and your budget! Being able to control your ad spend is beneficial. You will be amazed by how much reach you can achieve with a $25-$50 budget.

Facebook Boost is one tool many churches utilize. If your church wants to create awareness for an upcoming event at your church, consider 'Boosting' the post on Facebook. When 'Boosting' the post, you will select the goal you are trying to accomplish (e.g., increase engagement, drive people to your church website). The remaining steps involve selecting a target audience (e.g., gender, age, location) and identifying copy for the display button (e.g., learn more, sign-up). You will also have to set your total budget by determining the duration of time you would like to keep the post circulating (e.g., five days, ten days, 15 days). The system will give you an estimated number of people you can reach, depending on the spend.

The most common place your ad will appear on Facebook is in the newsfeed. However, it can also appear in the stories for the people you have targeted. To build a robust ad campaign for more detailed targeting, you should include a test using Ads Manager.

If your strategy requires you to advertise on Instagram, your church will need a Facebook Business Page. As you would on Facebook, you can promote an ad on Instagram directly through the app by using the 'Promote' feature. Add your church's URL if you want to drive people to your website to learn more about your ministries. You can then determine your target audience using demographics, location, their interest, etc.

The other option is to allow Instagram to promote your ad to people already engaging with your information. Again, you can set your budget and the duration of your promotion. Instagram Ads can appear in the feeds and stories of those targeted. Ads Manager is available for complex Instagram Ad Campaigns.

We have mentioned Twitter is a fast-moving social media platform. Twitter Ads provide tools, so the right audience views your tweets. Twitter Ads help create awareness, get others to engage with your posts, and obtain followers.

There are specific tools for each of these goals. Suppose you want to create awareness for a particular tweet. In that case, you can purchase an option to have your tweet appear in your target audience's timeline.

Tweet Engagements help to maximize the number of engagements with your tweets. A Follower's Campaign will allow you to acquire more followers on Twitter for your church. These are all tools designed to assist you in achieving your objectives on a fleeting platform.

Complete your Social Media Strategy, then consider the most helpful way to utilize Social Media Advertising. These tools will help you create awareness, expand your reach, and specifically target those you think will thrive at your church or those who you want to reach with a specific message.

These tools are available to help you meet the objectives you have set for your church. As with any campaign, it is essential to review the results through analytics to make improvements where needed and duplicate areas of success.

Social Media Advertising Worksheet

Your church would like to create awareness for your annual Easter play in the community. How would you utilize one of these platforms to expand the reach of the ad campaign?

1. Which ad platform will you use?

2. Who is your target audience?

3. What is your budget?

4. What type of ad would you run?

5. What timeframe would you run the ad?

New Ministry Positions for the Phygital Church

When considering ministry in a Phygital environment, there are additional roles for the church to consider. Meeting your Social Ministry goals will require time and commitment. A dedicated Social Ministry Team can help your church thrive in the Phygital space.

> *"A dedicated Social Ministry Team can help your church thrive in the Phygital space."*

Depending on your approach, and if you plan to create Facebook Groups, the following roles may be helpful. (Titles are suggestions. You should use what aligns best with the structure of your organization.)

Social Ministry Director: The responsibility in this role is to ensure the execution of the overall Social Media Strategy according to plan. This role will create and develop a consistent presence on the social media platforms selected by the church.

Qualification Considerations: Communications Background, Social Media Savvy

Social Ministry Minister: This person can be available when you are streaming your church services online. They can interact with your virtual audience and help to create online content, etc.
Qualification Considerations: Theology Background, Social Media Savvy

Social Ministry Hospitality Team: Just as there is a hospitality team/greeter in the physical church, one should be present in the online space. This team will greet people and interact with them when they come on your live feed. They will help to build online relationships.
Qualification Consideration: Conversation Starter

Social Ministry Ambassadors: These are people in your ministry who have a good pulse on the church mission and the direction of the church. They will represent your church online posting and sharing content.

Qualification Considerations: Social Media Savvy, Outgoing, Understands the church goals and missions

If you establish Facebook Groups for church ministries, you may consider having someone manage each group. The role will depend on the ministry establishing the group. Two or three leaders for each group can help foster conversation and relationships in the group.

Group Leaders should:
- Invite members to the group.
- Acknowledge new members.
- Assist with engagement and communication.

Examples of Ministry Groups:
- ***Social Ministry Youth Minister***
- ***Social Ministry Men's Leader***
- ***Social Ministry Women's Leader***

Social Ministry Positions Worksheet

1. List the new Social Ministry positions most appropriate for your church.

2. Identify congregants who are familiar with the pulse of your church. (Ambassadors)

3. Which of your church ministries have the potential to establish groups to form online communities?

Social Media Policy

Since a team of people will assist with your social media presence, creating a Social Media Policy is essential. Your Social Media Policy will provide guidelines for appropriate and inappropriate conduct while representing your church. These guidelines protect the church's reputation and integrity.

Your policy should provide information that will help team members maintain a positive reputation online. Encourage them to share church events and approved posts on their personal social media pages. Policies will guide you in dealing with potentially harmful comments. Although, on specific platforms, it is easier to delete the statement from the feed.

Other Phygital Resources

While they are not social media platforms, Zoom and Cisco WebEx are digital considerations. Churches use these platforms to meet in small groups and for worship services. Both platforms provide an opportunity to stream your services to social media.

Should your church continue worshipping using Zoom or WebEx, it is beneficial to stream to the online environment. If not, it is essentially closing your church doors to an audience of 3.96 billion people.

These resources provide an easy way to share and inspire people through your sermons. If you are already meeting in a virtual environment, it takes a few additional steps to "go" and make disciples.

Zoom / Cisco WebEx

When used for small groups, Zoom and Cisco WebEx allow people all over the country to join in your bible studies or morning devotionals. Harvest Church Plainfield, located in Plainfield, Illinois, was one church that utilized Cisco WebEx during the pandemic.

Bishop Nolan McCants began a morning devotion time called DayStart. During this time, online attendees would focus on a weekly theme and reflect on a different scripture each weekday morning. This gathering created community and connections for people all over the nation. These connections were necessary during a time when we could not physically be with one another.

People might have never met, encouraged, or learned from one another if they had not been in the virtual space, or by phone, with Bishop McCants. Relationships and friendships were formed, birthdays were celebrated, but most importantly, Disciples were made, and folks grew spiritually. Harvest will also have new members when they return indoors because these gatherings fostered connections and relationships.

Church Websites

Social Media platforms help to create awareness for your church. While they allow for a wealth of shared information in different formats, a church website remains vital. "According to Grey Matter Research, 17 million Americans who don't regularly attend church visited a church website."[12] Your website is an introduction to your church for many visitors. It also provides an opportunity to share relevant information that is not on your social media pages.

Having an engaging home page is crucial if you are driving traffic to your church website. Once there, you can share information about your ministry. List your ministries and outreach opportunities, so people in the community know how your church is impacting surrounding neighborhoods.

The pandemic has changed the hearts of many, and people may want to assist with the church's outreach. For those not on social media, your church website is critical. It is usually the first place people will visit once they search for your church online.

> *"For those not on social media, your church website is critical."*

Suppose the goal of your church is to create awareness. In that case, the ministries you have and how your church supports the beloved community will be essential to highlight. You must have a functional and optimized website that provides the information viewers are coming to find.

Lastly, consider tying your website to your social media feed. Many websites will allow you to display your newsfeed. This helps to create an integrated experience. If embedding your social media newsfeed is not an option from your website provider, add the social media icons where your church has a presence. Icons can make it easier for people on your website to connect with you on social media.

Reflections and Call to Action

The pandemic presented us with many obstacles. But as in all things, God provided direction and hope amid despair. We must acknowledge what has transpired because of the shift in introducing Christ in new and innovative ways. Social Ministry was a new undertaking for many churches. It provided a quick learning experience with benefits directly impacting the Kingdom of God.

Some people avoid being on Social Media because of the negativity that resides on many of these platforms. However, we are the light and salt of the world, even in the digital space. May we live in spaces that need light.

People are searching and looking for answers, and, for many, the digital space is where they turn because it is convenient. We have an opportunity to minister to people who might not visit our churches without having an online introduction.

We have many unbelievers who will continue to be so without our having shared the Good News. There are many people hanging onto hope, and the thread is getting thin, but we can give hope over these platforms.

The pandemic has provided us with an opportunity to see just how differently we could accomplish our goals if we were open to new ways of ministry. Many churches took a leap of faith into Social Ministry and have experienced the opportunity to reach the masses. Why would you want to retreat behind your church doors and not continue in this space? We are in a new season; it is time to approach ministry anew! The Phygital Church should become the new normal.

God has provided clergy with other means to reach those in need of hearing the Word. Social Ministry enables the Gospel to be shared with people who had not considered, or have not been previously driven, to come within the four walls of the church.

You are encouraged to continue as a Phygital Church. God has given us new and creative ways to reach people. May we continue to utilize them so we can meet people where they are. Now, go!

> *"God has given us new and creative ways to reach people. May we continue to utilize them so we can meet people where they are. Now, go!"*

This resource is not inclusive of all the platforms, tools, or features available for your use. (And they will continue to have updates.) The objective is to help you begin a strategic journey and be intentional in the Phygital environment.

You have a great start at creating a Social Media Strategy for your Social Ministry if you completed the worksheets along the way. So far, you've done the following:

- reflected on where you have been in the social media space
- selected the best social media platform(s) for your church based on demographics and characteristics of people that reside on the platform,
- defined your church's S.M.A.R.T. goals,
- identified metrics to monitor your progress,
- created key content to schedule, and
- strategized on using social media ads.

This is a great start! Add additional context to the information you have already discovered to reveal a fuller picture of the direction you will pursue. Combined with the efforts at your physical location, these details should assist your Social Ministry in meeting your church goals.

The following Appendix provides an example, at a high level, of a strategy with more context added.

Appendix
Sample Social Media Strategy

Church Name: A.B.C. Christian Church
Yearly Theme: Faith
Key Scripture:
For we walk by faith, not by sight. (2 Corinthians 5:7)

Background:
We realize our congregation, along with others, has just experienced an unexpected event. Members have lost loved ones, neighbors, and colleagues. Our church has also lost precious family members.

Despite what it looks like, we must remain faithful. God has not forgotten about us, and all promises remain true. While our days and the world have changed, God remains the same. We are a community of believers, ready to encourage others to believe and walk by faith.

During the pandemic, we utilized Facebook Live for Social Ministry. It was simple and provided a quick way to share with congregants. Post pandemic, we will need to finalize which options work best for recording in the sanctuary.

We also realize the pandemic has had a significant impact on those in our surrounding communities. We want to ensure we are extending our reach and touching the lives of our neighbors. It will be necessary to make those who reside close to our church aware of our resources.

Goals:
1. Create awareness for our church/ministries.
2. Provide information to help members and visitors grow spiritually.
3. Increase worship attendance.
4. Connect with people and expand our outreach opportunities in our community.
5. Create awareness among youth and young adults to grow ministries.

Additional Scriptures:

Hebrews 11:1,6, Matthew 17:20, Mark 11:22, Matthew 6: 34

Church Audit

Church Demographics:

Ages: 65+ =5%

       64-50 = 55%

       49-30 = 15%

       29-18= 15%

       17-5= 10%

Gender: Male: 48% Female: 52%

Ethnicities: Multi-cultural

Income: Mid-range $150K+ household

Location: Maywood County

Church Attributes:

Welcoming, Loving, Innovative, Understanding, Open-minded, Caring, Giving

Thriving Ministries:

Men's Ministry, Women's Ministry

Growing Ministries:

Youth Ministry, Young Adults Ministry

Social Media Audit

Social Media Baseline Results:

Fans: Women: 55% Men: 45%

Highest Age Percentages: Women: 45 – 55 years

Men: 45 – 55 years

Followers: 630 page-followers

Social Media Platform: Facebook

Content: Inspirational Images

People Currently Reaching: Women: 69% Men: 31%
 45-54 years of age

Day/Time Fans are online: Wednesday: 6 p.m., Thursday: 2 p.m., Saturday: 12 p.m.

Social Media Platforms:

Facebook:

Goal: Communicate with congregants and other online viewers to keep them encouraged.

Frequency: Once a week (outside of Facebook Live service on Sundays.)

Social Media Strategy

(This begins your strategy going forward)

Current Analysis:

We are currently on Facebook to keep the lines of communication open. We want to keep our congregants encouraged. We have noticed an uptick in visitors viewing and engaging during our Sunday Services.

Social Media Objectives:

We would like to extend our reach utilizing Social Media. The goal is to become more engaged with our audience on Facebook and have a presence on Instagram. We believe

Instagram will allow us to reach young adults, a growing ministry for our church.

As we prepare for ministry post-pandemic, we want to be more intentional about reaching out to our communities. The plan is to use Social Media to create awareness for our church and the ministries we offer. Social Ministry will allow us to introduce the Gospel in creative and compelling ways and encourage viewers with a range of frequently posted content. The ultimate goal is to grow God's Kingdom.

Social Media Goals

Primary Goal: Create awareness of our church/ministries.
S.M.A.R.T. Goals:
Create awareness in Q1 with informative/uplifting posts and drive traffic to our website for people to learn more about our church/ministries using links.
Measurement: Track website visits

Create awareness in Q2 by posting short videos of members sharing thoughts about ABC Church and utilize the hashtag #abcchurch.

Measurement: Track hashtags

Primary Goal: Share God's word to help members and visitors grow spiritually (through Social Ministry).

S.M.A.R.T. Goals:

Live stream Sunday morning worship services in Q1.

Measurement: monitor online viewership, feedback, and comments

Implement an online morning devotional lesson in Q2.

Measurement: Monitor online viewership, feedback, and comments

Target Audiences:

Facebook

- Women and Men: 18 – 49 years of age
- Ethnicity: All ethnicities
- People who reside within a 30-mile radius of the church

- All who engage with us online
- Those who are outside the Body of Christ and in search of answers

Instagram

- Young Adults: 12 – 29 years of age
- Ethnicity: All ethnicities
- All who engage with us online
- Those who are outside the Body of Christ and in search of answers

Social Media Platforms:

Facebook

Goal: Utilize the platform to share worship, create awareness and engagement.

Features: Facebook Live, Video Shares, Posting and Boost Feature

Frequency: Three times a week (outside of Facebook Live service on Sundays).

Instagram

Goal: use the platform to interact with youth and young adults. Create awareness and engagement.

Features: Video Content on Reels, Instagram Live, and I.G.T.V.

Frequency: Twice daily, three times a week.

Content:

Created and Curated

Created: We will utilize clergy and staff to create content.

All created content should speak in a tone that represents our church: Welcoming, Loving, Innovative, Understanding, Open-minded, Caring, Giving

Curated Resources: NPR, Contemplative Monk, The Christian Post, and other sources with relevant article topics.

Q1 Sample Content Calendar:

ABC Christian Church
Content Calendar

Thursday, February 4

Social Media Platform	Content	URL	Type	Image	Format	Time
Facebook	We welcome you to worship with us online or at 123 Front Street this Sunday as Pastor Carolyn begins a sermon series on Walking by Faith. Visit us at abcchurch.org for more information.	facebook.com/abcchurch	Created	Image of person that portrays faith	Graphic Post	2:00 PM
Instagram	Video: Youth Ministry Leader introduces the topic for Sunday's Sermon. Invite youth to bring a friend on Sunday or tune in on FB.	abcchurch	Created	N/A	IG Video	9:00 AM
Instagram	I will walk by faith even when I cannot see. 2 Corinthians 5:7	abcchurch	Curated	Engaging background image	Graphic Post	2:00 PM

ABC Christian Church
Content Calendar

Saturday, February 6

Social Media Platform	Content	URL	Type	Image	Format	Time
Facebook	Remember to join us tomorrow at 10 am CST as Pastor Carolyn begins a sermon series on faith. Live close to the church? Join us in worship service at 123 Front Street.	facebook.com/abcchurch	Created	Image of Pastor speaking	Graphic Post	12:00 PM
Facebook	For we walk by faith, not by sight. 2 Corinthians 5:7 ABC Church 123 Front Street, City, Town Visit us at abcchurch.org	facebook.com/abcchurch	Curated	Image of person walking	Graphic Post	4:00 p.m.
Instagram	Join us tomorrow on Facebook Live or at 123 Front Street as we talk about faith.	abcchurch	Created	Image representing faith	Graphic Post	9:00 AM
Instagram	Bring a friend and join us tomorrow at 10 am as we begin a new series on faith.	abcchurch	Created	Group of youth	Graphic Post	8:00 PM

ABC Christian Church
Content Calendar

Social Media Platform	Content	URL	Type	Image	Format	Time
		Sunday, February 7				
Facebook	Sunday Worship ABC Christian Church For we walk by faith, not by sight. 2 Corinthians 5:7	facebook.com/abcchurch	Curated	N/A	Facebook Live	10:00 AM
Instagram	Video: Young adults giving their thoughts from today's sermon.	abcchurch	Created	N/A	IG Video	1:00 PM
Instagram	The Lord is greater than the giants you face. 1 John 4:4 Have faith in His timing!	abcchurch	Curated	Image of youth	Graphic Post	5:00 PM

ABC Christian Church
Content Calendar

		Wednesday, February 10				
Social Media Platform	Content	URL	Type	Image	Format	Time
Facebook	Faith is a choice to trust God. ABC Christian Church Visit us at abccc.org	facebook.com/abcchurch	Created	Person thinking	Graphic Post	6:00 PM
Facebook	How to have a faith mindset - Article by Joyce Meyer	Your Mindset Matters | Everyday Answers - Joyce Meyer Ministries	Curated	N/A	N/A	4:00 PM
Instagram	Instagram Video: Youth Minister Mike creates a video to encourage youth and young adults given all they have been experiencing.	abcchurch	Created	N/A	IG Video	9:00 AM
Instagram	Faith, Family, Friends	abcchurch	Created	Image	Graphic Post	2:00 PM

Social Media Analytics:

Frequency: Weekly analytics review

ABC Church Objectives	Social Media Goal	Analytics to Review
Create awareness of church/ministries	Awareness	Reach / Impressions / Website Visits
Provide information to help members/visitors grow spiritually	Awareness/Engagement	Reach / Impressions / Website Visits
Increase worship attendance/engagement	Audience Growth Rate	Net New Followers/Total Audience x 100
Create awareness for outreach	Awareness	Reach / Impressions / Website Visits
Create awareness among youth/young adults	Awareness	Reach / Impressions / Website Visits

New Ministry Roles to Implement:

- Social Ministry Director: Adrienne Smith
- Social Ministry Minister: Rev. Darius Mitchell
- Social Ministry Hospitality Team: Alexis Adams, Sylvia Conway, Donovan Jones, and Chris Evans
- Social Ministry Ambassadors: Yolanda Smith, Nathaniel Parker, Linda Fuller

Facebook Groups: Women's Ministry

Bibliography

A. List. "TikTok Increases Video Length Limit from 60 seconds to Three Minutes." July 2, 2021, TikTok Increases Video Length Limit From 60 Seconds To Three Minutes (alistdaily.com), https://www.alistdaily.com/social/social-media-news-070721/

Backlinko. "Social Network Usage & Growth Statistics: How Many People Use Social Media in 2021?" Updated April 26, 2021, https://backlinko.com/social-media-users

Barna Research Group. "Current Trends in Virtual Attendance & Weekly Giving Amid Covid-19." Accessed April 7, 2020, https:www.barna.com/research/current-attendance-giving-trends/

Barna Research Group. "How technology is changing millennial faith." October 15, 2013, https://barna.com/research/how-technology-is-changing-millennial-faith

Iconosquare. "50 Important TikTok Statistics for 2021." March 30, 2021, https://iconosquare.com/50-important-tiktok-statistics-for-2021

Pew Research Center. "Mobile Fact Sheet, Who owns cellphones and smartphones." January 25 – February 8, 2021, Retrieved from https://www.pewresearch.org/internet/fact-sheet/mobile

Pew Research Center. "More Americans Than People in Other Advanced Economies Say Covid-19 has Strengthened Religious Faith." Accessed January 27, 2021, https://www.pewforum. org/2021/01/27/more-americans-than-people-in-other-advanced-economies-say-covid-19-has-strengthened-religious-faith/

Pew Research Center. "Social Media Use in 2021" April 7, 2021, https://pewresearch.org/internet/2021/04/07/social-media-use-in-2021/

Pew Research Center. "Teens, Social Media and Technology 2018.",May 31, 2018, https://pewresearch.org/internet/2018/5/31/teens-social-media-technology-2018

Reach Right. "37 Church Statistics You Need To Know For 2019. https://reachrightstudios.com/church-statistics-2019

Renderforest. "44 Video Marketing Statistics." December 17, 2020, https://www.renderforest.com/blog/video-marketing-statistics

Stout, Dustin. "Social Media Statistics 2021: Top Networks by the Numbers." 2021, https://dustinstout.com/social-media-statistics

Walla Room Media. "Tik Tok Statistics- Updated February 2021." Last updated February 6, 2021, https://wallaroomedia.com/blog/social-media/tiktok-statistics/

Endnotes

[1] Barna Group Current Trends in Virtual Attendance & Weekly Giving Amid Covid -19.
[2] Pew Research "More American Than People in Other Advanced Economies Say COVID-19 Has Strengthened Religious Faith."
[3] Backlinko.com social media users.
[4] Pew Research Center Mobile Fact Sheet, "Who owns cellphones and smartphones."
[5] Barna.com "How technology is changing millennial faith." Also, "Millennials Are Losing Their Religion, and Driving Massive ...."
[6] DustinStout.com "Social Media Statistics."
[7] Pew Research "Teens, Social Media, and Technology 2018."
[8] Iconosquare.com, "50 important TikTok Statistics for 2021."
[9] Alistdaily.com, "Tik Tok Increases Video Length Limit From 60 Seconds To Three Minutes."
[10] Wallaroomedia.com, "Tik Tok Statistics."
[11] Renderforest.com "44 Video Marketing Statistics."
[12] Reach Right. "37 Church Statistics You Need To Know For 2019.

www.ingramcontent.com/pod-product-compliance
Lightning Source LLC
Chambersburg PA
CBHW070932080526
44589CB00013B/1491